OVERCOMING ADVERSITY:
SHARING THE AMERICAN DREAM

SAMUEL L. JACKSON

MASON CREST PUBLISHERS
PHILADELPHIA

OVERCOMING ADVERSITY:
SHARING THE AMERICAN DREAM

OVERCOMING ADVERSITY:
SHARING THE AMERICAN DREAM

SAMUEL L. JACKSON

STACIA DEUTSCH AND RHODY COHON

MASON CREST PUBLISHERS
PHILADELPHIA

ABOUT CROSS-CURRENTS

When you see this logo, turn to the Cross-Currents section at the back of the book. The Cross-Currents features explore connections between people, places, events, and ideas.

Produced by OTTN Publishing, Stockton, New Jersey

Mason Crest Publishers
370 Reed Road
Broomall, PA 19008
www.masoncrest.com

First printing

1 3 5 7 9 8 6 4 2

Library of Congress Cataloging-in-Publication Data

Deutsch, Stacia.
  Samuel L. Jackson / by Stacia Deutsch and Rhody Cohon.
      p. cm. — (Sharing the American dream : overcoming adversity)
  Includes bibliographical references.
  ISBN 978-1-4222-0580-8 (hc) — ISBN 978-1-4222-0750-5 (pb)
  1. Jackson, Samuel L.—Juvenile literature. 2. Motion picture actors and actresses—United
States—Biography—Juvenile literature. I. Cohon, Rhody. II. Title.
  PN2287.J285D48 2008
  791.4302'8092—dc22
  [B]
                                        2008023428

OVERCOMING ADVERSITY:
SHARING THE AMERICAN DREAM

TABLE OF CONTENTS

CHAPTER ONE

WHAT'S IN A NAME?

In Hollywood, actors and actresses change their names all the time. They do it because a different name might read better on a movie marquee or sound more glamorous. A new name might also be easier for people to remember or pronounce.

For Sam Jackson, taking on a new name meant more than a flashy Hollywood identity. In 1991, when Jackson's world crumbled, he decided to change his name and his life. Sam Jackson, struggling actor and drug addict, became Samuel L. Jackson, the clean and sober rising star.

Hitting Bottom

Sam Jackson started using drugs in college. By the time he got the help he needed, he'd been an addict for more than 20 years. He was also an alcoholic. His wife, LaTanya Richardson, wanted him to go to a hospital and get help. Sam refused. He kept telling her that all the best actors and actresses had problems with drugs and alcohol. He would be okay, since someday he was going to be one of the greats. He could handle his problems by himself.

One day LaTanya came home to find her husband crumpled on the floor underneath their kitchen table. His eyes were closed.

Samuel L. Jackson is one of the most successful actors in Hollywood. But his climb to the top was not easy.

His head was tilted at a strange angle. His breathing was shallow. LaTanya called for help.

Getting Help

In 1991, Sam spent 28 days at a rehabilitation center in upstate New York. He finally admitted he had a problem. This wasn't easy, as he recalled in a 2003 interview with London's *Sunday Herald:*

> The worst day I've ever had was the first time I had to stand up in rehab. . . . My wife and my daughter were there and I had to stand up and say "Hi, my name is Sam and I am an addict," and look at them and see them look at me. That was pretty difficult.

After his treatment was finished, he wanted to get back to work right away. Sam had been building his acting career for almost 20 years. During that time, he had worked for a lot of directors and producers. He had played a number of small roles in the theater, on television, and in the movies. Before he went to rehabilitation, Jackson was working consistently, perhaps not in the big, breakout roles he hoped he would someday have, but he was earning a living as a working actor. After he returned home clean and sober, he decided to call around and tell the directors and producers he'd worked with in the past that he was a changed man. He was ready to start working again. It was difficult for Jackson. He quickly discovered that many people in the entertainment industry were reluctant to take a chance on an actor who'd had serious drug and alcohol problems.

It was Sam's friend Spike Lee who was willing to give him the opportunity he desperately needed. Lee was a well-respected young director. Sam had previously played small roles in two

Director Spike Lee poses for photographers at the 1991 Cannes Film Festival. At the world-famous film festival in France, Lee accepted a special award for Samuel L. Jackson, who had starred in his film *Jungle Fever.*

of Lee's movies, *School Daze* (1988) and *Do the Right Thing* (1989). Before his collapse, Sam had already agreed to act in Lee's latest movie, *Jungle Fever.* He was going to play the role of Gator Purify, the brother of the main character.

But when Sam went into the rehabilitation clinic, it appeared that Lee would have to find another actor. Sam didn't want to give up the part. He thought

READ MORE

To learn more about the career of Spike Lee, see page 44.

the role of Gator Purify would be perfect for him. Gator was a drug addict who was always begging for money to feed his habit. Sam called Spike Lee and pleaded, "Don't recast me—I've done all the research."

Sam knew firsthand the pain of addiction. He knew that he would be able to use that experience to create a believable character. Lee agreed to keep him in the film.

Before returning to work, though, Sam decided to change his name to Samuel L. Jackson. This would show that the drug- and alcohol-addicted Sam Jackson was dead and gone. Samuel L. Jackson was a new person, sober and ready to take on the world.

A Star Is Born

Movie critics loved *Jungle Fever*. It was very well received at one of the world's largest and most important film festivals, in Cannes, France. Early buzz was that the film would win the prestigious Palme d'Or Award for best film at Cannes. It didn't. Yet something amazing still happened at Cannes.

READ MORE

The Cannes Film Festival has been held annually for more than 60 years. For a brief description of the festival, turn to page 45.

The judges at Cannes recognized the brilliance of Samuel L. Jackson's performance in *Jungle Fever*. They wanted to honor him, but the Cannes festival awarded only two prizes for acting: one for best actor and the other for best actress. There was no prize for an actor who had played a supporting role in a movie. To get around this, the judges created an award especially for Jackson. They gave Samuel L. Jackson a one-time-only Special Jury Prize Award for Best Supporting Performance.

Samuel wasn't in France to receive the award. Spike Lee accepted for him. But from that day on, Samuel Jackson was in high demand for movie and television roles.

A New Man

Samuel used to think drugs and alcohol were just a normal part of an actor's world. But after going to rehab and winning the Special Jury Prize at Cannes, he realized he'd been wrong.

It was only after breaking his addiction to alcohol and drugs that Samuel L. Jackson found success as an actor and, more important, happiness.

"Amazingly, as soon as I stopped drinking and drugging," he said in a 2005 interview, "I became a successful actor. Hollywood called. The rest is history."

Now, with more than 80 movies under his belt, Samuel L. Jackson is known as one of the hardest-working actors in Hollywood. And, with more than 15 acting awards, he is also known as one of the best.

CHAPTER TWO

LOOKING FOR A WAY TO CHANGE THE WORLD

Samuel Leroy Jackson was born in Washington, D.C., on December 21, 1948. His parents separated when he was a baby. Sam's mother, Elizabeth, then took him to Chattanooga, Tennessee, where she was from. He lived there with her and his maternal grandparents.

It was as a child that Sam developed his love of the movies. He particularly liked westerns, monster movies, and adventure stories. He would go to the kid-friendly movies and cartoon features in the morning. Then, he would stay to see whatever the theater was showing in the afternoon. Around four in the afternoon, his mother would arrive and join him. Together they would watch the more adult, dramatic films, usually two in a row.

Seeing all those movies as a child had a huge impact on Samuel later as an actor. It made him strive to be in exciting movies that could capture people's interest and imagination. Spending his time in the theater made Sam very happy. And yet, at the same time, going to the movies also made him mad.

Chattanooga had many movie theaters, but Sam could only go to two: the Liberty or the Grand. That's because they were the only black theaters; the others were reserved for whites. Chattanooga was in the heart of the segregated South, where

Before the civil rights movement of the 1950s and 1960s, African Americans weren't allowed to use the same public facilities as whites in the South. Here a black man walks up the stairs to the "colored" entrance of a movie theater, Belzoni, Mississippi, circa 1939.

blacks were not permitted to go to the same schools, eat in the same restaurants, stay at the same hotels, or use any of the same public facilities as whites.

Sam grew up understanding but not liking the fact that there were different rules for blacks and whites. He also knew from an early age that the world shouldn't be this way. In a 2005 interview, he discussed his hard feelings about growing up in a segregated world:

> I had anger in me. It came from growing up suppressed in a segregated society. All those childhood

years of "whites only" places and kids passing you on the bus yelling. . . . There was nothing I could do about it then. I couldn't even say some of the things that made me angry—it would have gotten me killed. But, I had a dream of my own. I was determined to get out and make my family proud.

Getting an Education

Sam's grandparents valued education. They did everything they could to ensure that he got a good education, and he did what he could to make them proud. While other members of the family worked, he knew his only job was to attend school so that he could make something of himself. He rose to the occasion and brought home consistently good grades. He was also interested in music at school and played both the trumpet and the French horn. After school, when he wasn't doing homework, Sam enjoyed swimming and running. He was busy, but he always made time for his homework. Sam was such a good student that he made the honor roll in high school.

In keeping with his family's idea that he should be well educated in order to make something good of himself, Sam wanted to go to college after high school. He applied to Morehouse College in Atlanta. Morehouse was a highly respected school for black men, and Sam was accepted.

At Morehouse, Sam began to study to be a marine biologist. Unsure what career he wanted, he also studied architecture for a while. He did well in his

READ MORE

Morehouse College was founded right after the Civil War. See page 46 to learn more about the college's history and to read about some famous graduates.

classes and enjoyed campus life. Unfortunately, Sam Jackson would be expelled from school before he could get a degree.

An Angry Young Man

During Sam's third year of college, the great civil rights leader Martin Luther King Jr. was assassinated. It happened on April 4, 1968, in Memphis, Tennessee. King was himself a graduate of Morehouse College. Sam went to Dr. King's funeral in Atlanta to honor the leader's memory. Then he flew to Memphis to attend a protest march. When he returned to Morehouse, Sam was now determined to see some changes at the college.

At the time, Morehouse, even though it was a college for black students, had no African American studies program. Sam and a group of like-minded students—and some faculty members—thought this was wrong. They wanted to talk to the school's board of trustees about changing the curriculum. But the board refused to listen to their requests.

Sam Jackson and a group of his fellow students grew frustrated. Finally, in 1969, they decided to take matters into their own hands and stage a protest. They locked the board of trustees in a meeting room. The students then demanded that school officials hear their complaints. Obviously the board had no choice but to listen.

Eventually, Morehouse agreed to consider the students' demands, and the board was released. They had been trapped in the meeting room for about a day and a half. The takeover ended with no one getting hurt. But, as Samuel Jackson recalled in a 2005 interview, it could have turned out very differently. "We were buying guns," he said, "getting ready for an armed struggle."

Morehouse College threw out all the students involved in the school takeover. This included Sam Jackson, even though he had been a model student.

Civil rights leader Dr. Ralph Abernathy (center, at podium) addresses a crowd at a memorial service for Martin Luther King Jr., Morehouse College, Atlanta, Georgia, April 9, 1968. King, the most prominent leader of the civil rights movement, had been assassinated four days earlier. The event galvanized Sam Jackson, who at the time was a Morehouse student.

The incident fueled Elizabeth Jackson's fears that her son's anger might boil over. She understood that Sam had recently been drawn to the radical views of Stokely Carmichael, a founder of the Black Power movement. Carmichael believed that violence might be necessary to end white racism in America. Elizabeth Jackson worried that her son might be swept up in Stokely Carmichael's kind of radical violence.

Then, proving her right, the FBI showed up at her home in Atlanta. The agents warned her that if Sam didn't calm down, he would probably be dead within a year. Sam's mother wanted to protect him, so she decided that he needed to move far away. Getting him out of town was the only way she could think of to get him to stop hanging out with people she considered bad influences. Mrs. Jackson arranged for her son to live in Los Angeles.

READ MORE

Turn to page 47 to learn more about Stokely Carmichael and the Black Power movement.

Finding His Voice

While he was living in Los Angeles, Sam worked for Social Services. But even while living and working in L.A., Sam knew that he wanted to finish his college degree. After two years of cooling off, Sam was no longer the angry man he'd been when he left Chattanooga. He was ready to start again. He reapplied to Morehouse, and the college agreed to let him return. Sam returned to Morehouse College in Atlanta in 1971.

In addition to finishing his education, Sam wanted to work on a personal problem that had been plaguing him since childhood. For as long as he could recall, he'd had a terrible stutter. While in fourth grade at elementary school, Sam was so embarrassed by it that he refused to talk at all for the whole year. The first time he was in college, he had worked on improving his speech. But he still had trouble.

This time around, an instructor suggested that public speaking might help with his stutter. He was willing to try. He went to an audition for a college musical production.

Samuel L. Jackson and his wife, actress LaTanya Richardson, pose for photographers outside the Shrine Auditorium in Los Angeles before the 70th Annual Academy Awards, March 28, 1998. Samuel and LaTanya met while they were college students. They married in 1980.

Sam won a part in the play. And he discovered that acting and public speaking did help his stutter. But he also discovered something else: the romantic love of his life. LaTanya Richardson was a theater major at Spelman College, Morehouse's sister school. He fell head over heels in love with her at first sight. She was immediately attracted to him as well. "He was very, very fine," she recalled later. The two began dating.

Not only had Sam found the woman he loved, but he had also found inspiration in acting. He soon changed his major to drama. While at Morehouse, he cofounded an all-black acting company called Just Us Theater.

In 1972 Sam Jackson finally graduated from Morehouse and decided to pursue an acting career full time. He still saw racial injustices in the United States. He still believed that much about American society needed to be changed. But now he thought he could do his part to create a positive change through theater and film. "I decided that theater would now be my politics," he later explained. "It could enrage people and affect the way they think. It might even change some minds."

After college, and still living in Atlanta, Sam and LaTanya toured with a theater company called the Black Image Theater Company. Sam also performed in his first movie role. He played a character named Stan in a 1972 feature film called *Together for Days*. He also appeared in his first television commercial. It was for a fast food chain called Krystal Hamburgers. From there, he had other small television roles, including a part in a 1977 TV movie called *Displaced Person*. A year later, he appeared in *The Trial of the Moke*, a public television drama.

Sam knew that he needed to be in a city where there were more job possibilities for actors. In 1976 he and LaTanya decided to move to New York City together. They were married in 1980.

CHAPTER THREE

THE STRUGGLE TO BECOME AN ACTOR

Many young actors flock to New York City to pursue their dream of becoming a star. Sam Jackson was no different. He went to New York to look for acting jobs, but he didn't become a star right away.

In 1982 he and LaTanya Richardson had a daughter, Zoe. While Zoe was little, Sam struggled to make it in New York's glamorous theater district.

He joined both the Negro Ensemble Company and the New York Shakespeare Company. Although he worked regularly, the parts that he was offered were small, and the pay was low. He scrambled to make a living.

To support his family, Sam didn't get the traditional actor's job: working as a waiter in a restaurant. Instead he worked as a doorman at the Manhattan Plaza. This apartment building was home to many actors and actresses. As doorman, Sam met people with whom he would act in the future.

While performing at the New York Shakespeare Company, Sam met actor Morgan Freeman. The two became friends. Freeman, who is 10 years older, became Sam's mentor. He offered Sam advice and help in his career. Freeman convinced Sam that if he worked hard and kept auditioning for roles, he would someday become a successful actor.

The New York skyline. The city is a magnet for aspiring actors. Sam Jackson and LaTanya Richardson decided to move there in 1976 to pursue their acting dreams.

Even with Freeman's guidance, during the 1980s Sam Jackson was struggling to find his place in the acting world. He did whatever he could to stay connected to the theater. He felt that the best way to get his foot

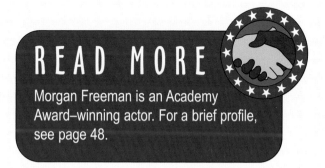

READ MORE

Morgan Freeman is an Academy Award–winning actor. For a brief profile, see page 48.

in the door and possibly get noticed by those in charge was to hang around and meet people. Sam built sets. He attended workshops. Most important, he went to auditions as often as he could.

In a 2006 PBS interview with Tavis Smiley, Samuel L. Jackson recalled:

> Actors act. I didn't wait tables. I didn't do all that other stuff. I acted. All the things that I learned to do at Morehouse like build sets, do costumes, hang lights, do all those other things, I did to support myself when I wasn't acting. When I had an audition, the people in the theater would go, "Good luck," not "Hey, who's going to wait my table?"

Sometimes it was difficult to keep pushing when the big parts just were not coming his way. When things weren't going well for him, Sam got depressed. He thought, as many people have before, that taking drugs and drinking alcohol would make him feel happier. They might even help him gain greater acceptance in the acting community.

Sam began smoking marijuana, but it did not improve his mood. He was sad all the time. The auditions were hard, and the rejections made him feel sorry for himself. Eventually, Sam progressed to stronger drugs, thinking those would help him feel better. He even thought the drugs would make him a better actor. Eventually, he started using a very addictive drug, cocaine.

A Few Small Roles

Sam Jackson did whatever he could to build his résumé. He was willing to work for television, the stage, or movies. He simply wanted to be an actor.

In 1984 Sam Jackson had an unusual job. He worked as a stand-in for Bill Cosby on the popular TV comedy *The Cosby Show*. Stand-ins walk through scenes, pretending to be the main actor

Bill Cosby on the set of his hugely popular television sitcom *The Cosby Show.* In 1984, Sam Jackson worked as Cosby's stand-in on the show.

before the actual shooting. This pre-shoot walk-through allows the director and technicians to arrange lighting and camera angles without wasting the star's time. Being a stand-in, although it was a job in the right industry, wasn't what Sam wanted. But at least it was a job.

In the Theater

On the live theater stage, Sam wasn't landing the roles he wanted either. But he believed the theater was where actors really learned the craft, so he stuck with it while he was trying to break into TV. He did get a few interesting parts in theater shows.

Sam was in productions of *The Piano Lesson* and *Two Trains Running,* two plays by the influential African American playwright August Wilson. The shows played off-Broadway. *The Piano Lesson* went on to win a Pulitzer Prize.

Unfortunately, when *Two Trains Running* moved up to Broadway, another actor was hired to take over the role Sam had played off-Broadway. Needless to say, Sam was terribly disappointed. His drug use became even worse while he sat backstage on Broadway as the understudy, watching another actor play the role he used to star in.

READ MORE

Turn to page 49 to learn about New York City's Broadway theater district.

In 1981 Sam played the role of army private Louis Henson in an off-Broadway production of *A Soldier's Play*. A fellow cast member, Denzel Washington, would rocket to stardom as a result of his work in the Pulitzer Prize–winning play. But Sam didn't have the same sort of luck. His luck came in a different way.

One night, after a performance, Sam was introduced to a man who would eventually change his life, making him the big star he hoped to become. That man was Spike Lee. He didn't know it yet, but Spike Lee was someday going to be a famous African American director, producer, and writer.

In a *New York Times* interview, Samuel Jackson recalled the meeting. "He told me he was a Morehouse alumnus, that he was at NYU [New York University] film school, da-da-da. He was going to, um, be a filmmaker. He said when he started to make films, he would love for me to be in his movies."

At the time, of course, Sam Jackson had no idea how this meeting would eventually affect his career. In the meantime, he continued to struggle as an actor. He continued to drink heavily and abuse drugs, thinking that this would somehow help.

Noteworthy Movie Roles

Even though times were hard, Sam Jackson continued to pursue his dream. He took smaller television and stage roles, hoping they would lead to larger parts. He also continued to audition for

Sam Jackson became a drug addict while toiling to establish his acting career.

movies. Before his breakout performance in Spike Lee's *Jungle Fever*, Sam had a number of small roles in movies.

His first film role after moving to New York was in Milos Forman's 1981 movie, *Ragtime*. "My first big film where I mistakenly thought I was off and running on my way to Hollywood was *Ragtime*," Samuel Jackson recalled in 1991. "I was gang member #3. That was one of the first rude awakenings I got about the film business itself." Sam realized that the acting world was not going to be easily won over. Roles were not simply going to land at his feet just because he'd performed in one film. He was going to have to work very hard if he wanted to succeed.

After *Ragtime,* he continued to get small roles in movies. He played the role of George in a 1987 made-for-TV movie adaptation of Harriet Beecher Stowe's *Uncle Tom's Cabin,* costarring Bruce Dern. He was a robber in *Coming to America* (1988), with Eddie Murphy and Arsenio Hall. In *Sea of Love* (1989), starring Al Pacino, his role was so small that hardly anyone noticed. He played a taxi dispatcher in Alan Alda's movie *Betsy's Wedding* (1990). In *Exorcist III* (1990), he appeared in a dream sequence. In Martin Scorsese's *Goodfellas* (1990), he was a crazy lowlife.

In all, Sam Jackson had acted in about 20 movies by 1990. Many of these films were well received by critics, but Sam's parts weren't big enough to push his career to the next level. In fact, most of the films didn't even list his name in the credits.

With drugs and alcohol beginning to take over his life, Sam's career was on shaky ground. He was starting to develop a reputation for being difficult. It's often hard for new actors to get jobs when they are out of control, even if they are talented.

"I had never once been onstage without a substance in my body," Samuel L. Jackson admitted in a 2005 interview. "I rehearsed that way. I performed that way. Then I went too far."

At rock bottom in 1991, Sam Jackson realized that he needed to make a major change in his life. "There is no formula," he told Oprah Winfrey in 2006, speaking of rehabilitation. "You just have to kind of make up your mind that you're sick and tired of doing what you're doing and you want to change your life."

CHAPTER FOUR

TAKING CONTROL

Sam Jackson had worked for the acclaimed director, producer, and writer Spike Lee a couple of times since they first met backstage at *A Soldier's Play*, in 1981. Lee cast Sam in a small part for his 1988 film, *School Daze*. The two worked well together, and Lee asked Sam to return for a bigger part in his 1989 movie, *Do The Right Thing*. When Spike Lee likes an actor or actress, he is known to hire that person again and again for other movies.

When Samuel L. Jackson appeared in Spike Lee's 1991 movie, *Jungle Fever*, it marked a turning point in his career. For his role as Gator Purify, a dangerous drug addict, Samuel received a special award at the Cannes Film Festival. He suddenly started receiving the attention he had been looking for. Directors and producers were calling to ask him to appear in their movies. After Cannes, Samuel L. Jackson got all the acting work he could handle.

And for the first time, Samuel could pick the kind of roles he wanted. He no longer had to take just about any role that came his way. At first, he tried many different kinds of roles. Gradually, he tested his skills and slowly figured out what kinds of movies he liked to act in best. Since his performance in *Jungle Fever*,

Samuel has been in an astounding number of movies. He averages about five films per year.

In 1992, he was in the inner-city drama *Juice* and a psychothriller called *White Sands*. He also appeared in *Patriot Games, Jumpin' at the Boneyard,* and *Fathers and Sons.* After playing many dramatic roles, he decided to try his hand at comedy. Samuel starred in the 1993 comedies *National Lampoon's Loaded Weapon 1* and *Amos & Andrew.*

In fact, 1993 was a banner year for Samuel. He also appeared in *Menace II Society, Jurassic Park,* and the crime thriller *True Romance,* which was written by a newcomer on the Hollywood scene, Quentin Tarantino.

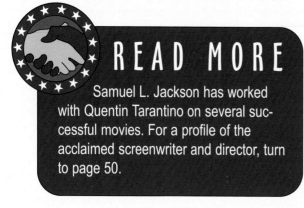

READ MORE

Samuel L. Jackson has worked with Quentin Tarantino on several successful movies. For a profile of the acclaimed screenwriter and director, turn to page 50.

Samuel was in some other notable films in the 1990s. In 1995, he starred with veteran actor Bruce Willis in *Die Hard with a Vengeance.* Internationally, it was the top grossing film of the year. He received a Golden Globe nomination and an NAACP Image Award in 1996 for his role in the film *A Time To Kill.* He was also in *The Long Kiss Goodnight* (1996) and *The Negotiator* (1998).

Samuel discovered that he especially liked to play tough guys and villains. Often these roles had him using a gun, and his characters cursed a lot.

Some critics have complained about the characters Samuel L. Jackson plays. But, as Samuel told the *New York Daily News* in 2000, "I have a very hard edge, I'm cynical, and I have that kind of sarcastic thing going for me in my real life. . . . So, it's pretty natural for me to play guys like that."

Above: Samuel L. Jackson with director Quentin
Tarantino, 1997. Inset: a poster for Tarantino's *Pulp Fiction*. Samuel's career
received a huge boost after he was cast as a hit man in the 1994 movie.

Samuel's interest in the gritty side of life and his attraction to "cuss 'em and kill 'em" roles led him to work with Quentin Tarantino again. By 1994, Tarantino was no longer only a screenwriter but had also become a movie director. Tarantino remembered Samuel from his earlier performance in 1993's *True Romance.* "He has given me roles I can fill out," Samuel said of the acclaimed director.

> I love the way he writes and I love the people he has saying those words. They're guys I know in a very real sort of way and it's an opportunity to be as theatrical as you can possibly be in a film and still do people that have depth, move the story along, and have an impact on the audience.

In Tarantino's 1994 film *Pulp Fiction,* Samuel played a hit man. His performance earned him an Academy Award nomination for Best Supporting Actor. He didn't win the Oscar. But he did win other honors for his role, including an award for best actor in a supporting role from BAFTA, the British Academy of Film and Television Arts.

Samuel again worked with Tarantino on *Jackie Brown.* The 1997 movie had a star-studded cast that included Pam Grier, Robert De Niro, Chris Tucker, and Bridget Fonda. Samuel played an arms dealer. Again, he was recognized for his fine performance. He won Best Actor honors at the Berlin International Film Festival.

Science Fiction and Star Wars

In 1998, Samuel shared the screen in a new movie with two of Hollywood's biggest stars: Dustin Hoffman and Sharon Stone.

The movie was the science fiction thriller *Sphere,* and Samuel played a scientist. He realized that he liked acting in science fiction films. After hearing rumors around Hollywood that there was a big new science fiction movie under way, Samuel decided that he wanted to be in it. And soon he would get his desire fulfilled.

During a television interview in England, Samuel revealed that he admired George Lucas, the creator of the very popular *Star Wars* series. Three *Star Wars* movies had already been filmed, and Lucas was preparing to shoot another. It would be a prequel. In other words, the story would take place before the events depicted in the other movies in the series. In the interview, Samuel told the reporter that he'd like to be in the newest *Star Wars* movie.

George Lucas saw Samuel L. Jackson's TV interview. Lucas called and offered the actor a part in *Star Wars: Episode One— The Phantom Menace.* But he didn't tell Samuel what that part would be.

Samuel didn't care what role Lucas wanted him to play, as he told the magazine *Jet:*

> George Lucas told me, "You know, I'm not writing a lot of real good human parts in this movie. I know you're a good actor, but you may end up going, "Look out! Run!" And all I'll be telling you is, "Go this way. Run." And I said, "I don't care. I'll do anything. I just want to be in the movie."

Samuel told Lucas that he would even be willing to be a storm trooper or wear a mask and act the part of an alien. He didn't care. He was such a huge *Star Wars* fan that any role would have been okay.

Samuel L. Jackson as Jedi master Mace Windu. Playing the character in the three *Star Wars* prequels was a dream come true for Samuel. The distinctive color of Windu's light saber was Samuel's idea.

Until the day he arrived on the set, Samuel didn't even know if he would have a speaking part. He didn't know whether he would be covered head to toe in a costume. When he finally discovered that he was going to play the Jedi knight Mace Windu, Samuel was excited. "This has been the kind of year where I've worked with Dustin Hoffman

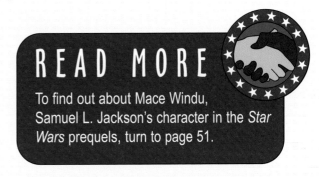

READ MORE

To find out about Mace Windu, Samuel L. Jackson's character in the *Star Wars* prequels, turn to page 51.

and Robert De Niro," he told the *New York Times*, "and all of a sudden I'm standing on a set doing scenes with Yoda. I said to myself, 'I've arrived.'"

Many others also believed that Samuel L. Jackson had arrived. It is not every day that someone says in an interview what they would like and then actually gets it.

Samuel would appear in all three *Star Wars* prequels. Much to his delight, he got to recite the immortal line from the *Star Wars* movies, "May the Force be with you."

The Phantom Menace made more than $28 million the day it was released. This was the highest one-day gross for a film in 1999. But for Samuel L. Jackson, that was secondary. The thrill of playing Mace Windu had been a high point of his acting career.

In *Star Wars Episode Two—Attack of the Clones* (2002), the first appearance of Mace Windu's light saber created a swirl of controversy among die-hard *Star Wars* fans. Mace's saber was purple, a color not seen before in any of the previous movies. Some fans suggested that the color had a mystical meaning. Samuel confessed that he had suggested the purple light saber simply because it would "look cool." Since the saber color was added later, after the actual filming, Samuel himself was

A sure sign the actor has arrived: a beaming Samuel L. Jackson at the dedication of his star on Hollywood's fabled Walk of Fame, June 16, 2000.

surprised to see it. He hadn't known that Lucas took his advice to heart and had given him a light saber that set him apart from the other Jedi knights.

A Star and Some Prints

Samuel had entertained millions of fans with his many movie roles. He had also won praise from film critics. He'd been nominated for—and won—a variety of acting awards.

And in 2000, he received one of the entertainment industry's most visible symbols of success. Samuel was awarded a star on Hollywood's famous Walk of Fame. His star can be found at 7018 Hollywood Boulevard.

In 2006, when he was 57 years old, Samuel also got to place his hand and feet prints permanently in the cement in front of Grauman's Chinese Theatre, also on Hollywood Boulevard. Samuel was only the seventh African American, out of 191 actors, honored with prints at the theater.

CHAPTER FIVE

MORE THAN A MOVIE STAR

By the year 2000, Samuel L. Jackson was a world-renowned actor whose services were always in demand. Although he was now financially secure, he continued to work at a surprisingly ambitious pace, averaging nearly four movies per year.

In 2000, Samuel costarred with Bruce Willis in *Unbreakable*, a suspense thriller by writer and director M. Night Shyamalan. That same year, he starred in *Rules of Engagement* and played the title role in *Shaft*. Those last two films were both shown at the Deauville Film Festival in France. At the festival, Samuel, who was 51 at the time, received a Lifetime Achievement Award.

In 2001, Samuel starred in *The 51st State*. The following year, he appeared in *xXx*. In 2002, Samuel reprised his role as Mace Windu in *Star Wars: Episode Two—Attack of the Clones*. More films followed, and in 2004, Samuel lent his voice to the character of Frozone in Disney's animated movie *The Incredibles*.

In 2005, Samuel L. Jackson played a basketball coach in the huge box-office success *Coach Carter*. The movie was screened at the opening night of the Palm Springs Film Festival, where Samuel was honored with a Career Achievement Award and Best Actor. He also garnered an NAACP Image Award.

Samuel L. Jackson mugs it up with the character Frozone at a party for the premiere of *The Incredibles,* October 24, 2004. Samuel voiced the character in the Disney movie.

The year 2005 also saw the release of *Star Wars: Episode Three—Revenge of the Sith.* Samuel knew that his character, Mace Windu, was going to die in this film. He requested that director George Lucas kill him off in a way befitting a Jedi of his standing. That, and he wanted to keep his light saber.

By the end of 2005, *The Guinness Book of World Records* listed Samuel L. Jackson as the star whose movies had grossed the most money at the box office. Samuel's total, $3.5 billion, put him ahead of Harrison Ford ($3.3 billion) and Tom Hanks ($3.1 billion).

Time will tell whether Samuel can retain his position as number one. But his much-anticipated role as Nick Fury in a sequel to 2008's popular *Iron Man,* a movie based on Marvel Comics characters, certainly won't hurt his chances.

Because of the incredible number of movies in which he has appeared, Samuel L. Jackson has been dubbed "Hollywood's hardest-working actor." Julianna Margulies, who costarred with Samuel in *Snakes on a Plane,* told an interviewer, "All Sam does

Samuel L. Jackson walks the red carpet before the premiere of *Snakes on a Plane,* August 17, 2006.

is work. I asked him, 'When do you ever sleep?' . . . He says, 'I'll sleep when I'm dead.'"

Never Mind the Critics

Though he has achieved fame and success as an actor, Samuel L. Jackson has received his share of negative reviews. For example, according to an article in the *Sunday Herald* of London, one American critic suggested that if all the swearing were removed from *The 51st State*, the film would be only 10 minutes long. Other Samuel Jackson vehicles, like *Snakes on a Plane* and *Black Snake Moan* (both released in 2006), have been almost universally panned by the critics.

Samuel L. Jackson has a reputation for looking up reviews and comments about his work on the Internet. He told Tavis Smiley:

> I will pull a critic up when I meet him and say, "You wrote so and so, so and so about the last film that I was in. Why did you feel that way? What about the film bothered you or what about my particular character disturbed you to the point that you had to say something like that?"

Critics can say whatever they want about Samuel L. Jackson, but the movie-going public still loves his work. Each new release is seen by millions of fans.

A New Addiction

Hollywood's hardest-working actor does find time to pursue other passions, however. In fact, Samuel L. Jackson has found a new, positive addiction. Whenever he signs up to star in a new movie, Samuel has a clause written into his contract that allows him time off for golf. Film producers are also expected to secure him temporary membership at a club near the filming location.

Samuel claims an eight handicap, quite respectable for an amateur golfer. He has played on some of the best courses in the world, including St. Andrews in Scotland. One of the most exciting golf moments for Samuel was when the actor played at St. Andrews with professional golf champion Tiger Woods. He told the *New York Daily News,* "Golf is the one game where every mistake you make you're responsible for. Nobody is playing defense, nobody is throwing the ball at you. Everything you do you have the responsibility for. It's relaxing to me. And gold courses are really beautiful places to hang out."

READ MORE

St. Andrews is considered the birthplace of golf. For details, turn to page 52.

In a 1996 interview with the magazine *MovieMaker,* Samuel said, "My new drug is golf. It's my drug of choice."

King of Cool

When Oprah Winfrey called Samuel L. Jackson the "King of Cool" in a 2006 interview, he replied, "It never occurs to me to leave home and say, 'I've got to be cool today' . . . I have a certain amount of confidence in who I am and what I'm capable of doing. I'm very fun loving and I like to laugh a lot, and I think people find that cool."

Samuel expanded on this in a later interview with *USA Today.* "I don't consider myself cool," he admitted. "If you were to go back thirty-five, forty years and talk to people I went to high school with, they'd tell you, 'Hell, he wasn't cool.' I've been fortunate to portray some characters who are cool under fire, who say interesting and cool things and who look a specific way."

Samuel L. Jackson swings his driver at the Alfred Dunhill Links Championship, a pro-amateur golf tournament held in Carnoustie, Scotland, October 4, 2007. Samuel is an avid golfer.

And yet, the nickname King of Cool *does* suit Samuel L. Jackson quite well. It's a nickname that reflects the kind of characters he likes to play: calm, collected, and bad to the bone. No longer the politically charged, drug-addicted youth he once was, Sam Jackson is now Samuel L. Jackson, successful, award-winning, and happy actor.

"I think I've made my family proud," he told an interviewer. "My wife says I've finally grown into the man she always knew I was going to be."

Samuel L. Jackson, "the King of Cool," 2007.

Samuel L. Jackson Makes Friends with Sam Jackson

A reporter for ESPN once asked Samuel L. Jackson about the difference between Samuel L. Jackson and Sam Jackson. The actor replied:

> They're the same guy. I try to treat everybody the same way, and I'm still the same guy I always was. Some people know me by one name or the other, but it doesn't make much difference to me. People who know me well usually call me Sam. One derivative of my name I really don't like, though, is Sammy. Other than that, I'll take all the rest of 'em.

The reporter then asked if Samuel has any other nickname. He answered, "Some friends call me Big Jack."

Samuel L. Jackson, Sam Jackson, Big Jack, or the King of Cool—they are all the same guy. He is a man who beat the odds, overcoming drug and alcohol abuse. He worked his way to the top—and has stayed there—in an industry in which success is not only extremely difficult but often also fleeting. For all his hard work and perseverance, Samuel L. Jackson has become a movie megastar.

Spike Lee

Spike Lee ranks as one of the most important figures in American filmmaking today. He is a director, producer, writer, and actor.

Lee was born in 1957 in Atlanta, Georgia. While a student at Morehouse College, he discovered a love of film. He decided to get a graduate degree in film at New York University (NYU).

In 1986, after graduating from NYU, Lee made his first feature-length movie. *She's Gotta Have It* was set in a black college. The film cost just $175,000 to make, but it went on to earn more than $7 million at the box office.

Lee followed up with a string of films that attracted a lot of attention. These included *Do the Right Thing* (1989), which explored race relations. Lee wrote the screenplay for the film, which was nominated for an Academy Award.

Malcolm X (1992) was a biopic. It was about a black leader who was murdered in 1965.

In addition to dramatic movies, Spike Lee has directed commercials, music videos, and documentary films. His 1997 documentary *4 Little Girls* was about the bombing of a Baptist church in Birmingham, Alabama, in 1963. Lee was nominated for an Academy Award for Best Director for this film.

Acclaimed movie director Spike Lee, photographed in 1991, the year *Jungle Fever* was released.

Cannes Film Festival

Cannes is a seaside city in southern France. It has only about 80,000 permanent residents. But every year, for two weeks in May, the city's population doubles as thousands of actors, directors, producers, and journalists travel to the city for its famous film festival.

In 1939, the French minister for Public Instruction and the Arts proposed the international film festival. But World War II broke out that year and lasted until 1945, so the first festival was not held until 1946.

In the beginning, the festival was simply a place where tourists came to see films. Prizes were given for nearly every movie shown. As the festival grew, the prizes became more important. Now there are only nine prizes awarded. The Palme d'Or Award, the most prestigious, is given for best feature film. There are also prizes for direction, screenwriting, and acting.

Over the years, the Cannes Film Festival has become a significant place for movie studios to show their new films. Each year hundreds of films from all over the world are shown at the Cannes Film Festival, and winning at Cannes is a great honor.

Each year, the French resort town of Cannes hosts a world-renowned film festival.

Morehouse College

Morehouse is an all-male, historically black college. It was founded in 1867, just two years after the Civil War. At the time, the school was called the Augusta Institute. Its mission was to educate black men as ministers and teachers. The school underwent a couple of name changes before it became Morehouse College in 1913.

Over the years, Morehouse expanded its mission and the courses it offered. Today, Morehouse offers 26 majors in three academic divisions. The school has about 3,000 students.

Morehouse has produced many famous graduates, but none is more notable than civil rights leader Martin Luther King Jr. King graduated from Morehouse in 1948. He won the Nobel Peace Prize in 1964.

Fellow Morehouse alum Maynard Jackson was elected mayor of Atlanta in 1973. This was the first time an African American became mayor of a southern city. Jackson graduated from Morehouse in 1956.

Dr. David Satcher graduated from Morehouse in 1963. He went on to become surgeon general of the United States (1998–2001).

Movie director Spike Lee is a 1979 Morehouse graduate. His friend Samuel L. Jackson got his degree from the school seven years earlier.

This statue of civil rights leader Martin Luther King Jr. stands on the campus of Morehouse College in Atlanta, Georgia. King graduated from Morehouse in 1948.

Stokely Carmichael and the Black Power Movement

Stokely Carmichael was a leader in the civil rights movement of the 1960s. He worked hard to end segregation. He participated in sit-ins and was arrested many times during the struggle for racial equality.

By the mid-1960s, Carmichael became disillusioned with the tactics of civil rights leaders such as Dr. Martin Luther King Jr., who believed in changing society through nonviolent means. Carmichael began speaking about another path. He called his movement Black Power. He said that blacks should have pride in their heritage. They should stop trying to get ahead in the "white" world. They should be self-reliant.

Black Power was not a new idea. But Carmichael held the idea up as an alternative to the mainstream civil rights movement.

Some Black Power supporters thought that the best way to reach their goals was through violence. Others tried to work through the political system.

In the end, Stokely Carmichael's radical politics made him a target for the government. Fearing assassination, Carmichael and his wife moved to Africa in 1969. He died of cancer in 1998 in Conakry, Guinea.

Stokely Carmichael gives a speech, July 1, 1967. Carmichael was a founder of the militant Black Power movement, which advocated the use of violence (if necessary) to secure equal rights for African Americans.

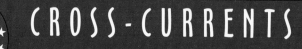

Morgan Freeman

Actor and director Morgan Freeman is one of the most respected people in Hollywood. He has won an Academy Award, a Screen Actors Guild Award, and a Golden Globe.

Freeman has more than 50 films to his credit. But he got his start on television. He appeared on the PBS children's show *The Electric Company* from 1971 to 1977.

He was nominated for an Academy Award for his role in the 1987 movie *Street Smart*. After that, the roles kept coming.

In 1990, Freeman played a chauffeur in *Driving Miss Daisy*. He was nominated for another Academy Award for his performance.

In *The Shawshank Redemption* (1994), Freeman played an aging prisoner. Again he earned an Academy Award nomination.

The fourth time Freeman was up for an Academy Award, he finally won. That was for the role of ex-boxer Eddie Dupris in the 2004 film *Million Dollar Baby*.

In addition to his skill as an actor, Freeman has a smooth, deep voice. This has led to work as a narrator. Freeman's narration credits include the 1996 IMAX film *Cosmic Voyage* and the 2005 National Geographic documentary *March of the Penguins*.

Morgan Freeman at the 45th Golden Globe Awards, January 23, 1988. The veteran actor served as a mentor to Samuel L. Jackson.

Broadway

The Broadway theater district of New York City is a relatively small area in the heart of Manhattan Island. It includes about 40 professional theaters. Nearly every night, thousands of people see plays on Broadway. Each year, more than $1.5 billion worth of tickets are sold for Broadway shows.

New York's first theatrical performances began in 1750. The theater held 280 people. It wasn't in the area that is today known as Broadway. But the theater was popular. And this spurred other theaters to open in lower Manhattan (the southern part of the island).

As the city grew, theaters began being built farther north on the island, where land was cheaper. By the early 1900s, theaters started opening in the area that is today known as the Broadway theater district. This is located between 42nd and 53rd Street, and between 6th and 9th Avenue.

New shows arrive on Broadway regularly. The most popular remain for a long time. In 2006, the musical *Phantom of the Opera* took the crown for the longest-running Broadway show, with 7,486 performances.

Broadway, one of New York's most famous thoroughfares, runs through the city's storied theater district.

Quentin Tarantino

In 1992, a little-known writer and director made a big splash at the Sundance Film Festival in Utah. He was Quentin Tarantino, and his movie was called *Reservoir Dogs*. The film quickly became a cult classic.

Two years later, Tarantino directed and cowrote *Pulp Fiction*. He was catapulted into fame when Pulp Fiction received seven Academy Award nominations and won for Best Original Screenplay. It also won the coveted Palme D'Or Award at the 1994 Cannes Film Festival.

Tarantino was born in Tennessee and dropped out of high school to become an actor. At 22, he moved to California and took a job at a local video store. There he watched hundreds of movies and learned everything he could about films.

Quentin Tarantino has won fame as a screenwriter and director.

In a 1994 interview with Charlie Rose, Tarantino remarked that his job at Video Archives in Hermosa Beach was where he learned about movies. "And what was funny about that job was the fact that . . . people said, 'Oh, so that's kind of like your film school.'"

From his beginning as a film watcher, Tarantino turned into a filmmaker. He has directed many feature films and television shows. He has done cinematography and is a prolific writer and producer. Tarantino also helps bring small, foreign films to theaters through his production company, Quentin Tarantino Presents . . .

Mace Windu

Mace Windu, played by Samuel L. Jackson, is one of the unforgettable characters in George Lucas's *Star Wars* movies. The character appeared in all three prequel movies, beginning with 1999's *The Phantom Menace* and continuing through *Attack of the Clones* (2002) and *Revenge of the Sith* (2005).

As a senior member of the Jedi High Council, Mace Windu is a prominent leader and respected elder. His opinion carries great weight in Council decisions. He is a master Jedi, similar in education to Yoda.

Windu believes in the power of words over action. He understands Jedi philosophy and knows of the ancient prophecy about a Chosen Jedi who could some day bring balance to the Force. He is uncertain, however, whether Anakin Skywalker is the Chosen One. Windu thinks that Anakin has too much power for a boy his age and is mistrustful of him.

His fears are confirmed when Anakin aligns himself with Darth Sidious, a dangerous Sith Lord. When Mace Windu has Sidious at his mercy, Anakin enters the fight, defending the Sith Lord.

In the ensuing battle, Anakin fights Mace Windu and, in a dramatic turn, cuts off the master's light saber hand, leaving him vulnerable. Sidious then unleashes his deadly energy at Mace Windu, propelling him out a window to plummet to his death.

Samuel L. Jackson as Mace Windu. This publicity photo, from 2002, is for *Star Wars: Episode II—Attack of the Clones.*

St. Andrews Golf Course

St. Andrews, Scotland—where Samuel L. Jackson had the pleasure of playing a round with legendary golfer Tiger Woods—is where the game of golf first developed. It is thought that people first started playing golf at St. Andrews between A.D. 1350 and 1400.

The town of St. Andrews is older still. By the eighth century A.D., there was a religious community in the area, and in the 1100s the town was officially founded. A university opened in St. Andrews in the early 1400s. Beginning in 1457, three successive kings of Scotland banned golf because it was seen as frivolous and took young men away from more worthwhile activities, such as church attendance. But golf would flourish in Scotland all the same.

Today lovers of golf have seven courses at St. Andrews from which to choose. The best known, however, is the Old Course. In 2005, *Golf Digest* magazine ranked it as the greatest course in the world outside the United States.

The Old Course appears in official records by 1552. A license from that year mentions that people were allowed to "play golf" there. At the time, the course consisted of just 12 holes. It wasn't until 1863, more than three centuries later, that the Old Course changed to the standard 18 holes. It has since been a mecca for golf aficionados from all over the world.

On the property sits the Royal and Ancient Golf Club of St. Andrews. The club does not own the property but is one of many clubs allowed to have facilities there. Until 2004, the Royal and Ancient Golf Club was the ruling international authority over golf. At that time, the club turned over the responsibility to a group called R&A, which today

monitors the game and maintains golf courses, equipment, and tournaments. The R&A has authority all over the world, except in the United States, where the United States Golf Association (USGA) sets the rules for golfers.

A view of St. Andrews, where the game of golf first developed.

Chronology

1948: Samuel Leroy Jackson is born on December 21 in Washington, D.C.

1969: Participates in a sit-in to protest policies at Morehouse College in Atlanta, Georgia. Is expelled from the school.

1971: After living and working in Los Angeles, returns to Morehouse College to finish his studies.

1972: Graduates from Morehouse College with a degree in dramatic arts.

1976: Moves to New York City to pursue a career in acting.

1980: Marries actress LaTanya Richardson.

1981: Meets Spike Lee while working as an understudy on the Broadway production of *A Soldier's Play*.

1982: Daughter, Zoe, is born.

1984: Works as Bill Cosby's stand-in on the TV sitcom *The Cosby Show*.

1991: Enters a rehabilitation center for drug and alcohol addiction; wins special Best Supporting Actor award for the film *Jungle Fever* at the Cannes Film Festival.

1994: Receives international acclaim for role in Quentin Tarantino's movie *Pulp Fiction*.

1999: Appears in the first of three *Star Wars* prequels as Mace Windu.

2000: Awarded star on Hollywood's Walk of Fame.

2004: Performs the voice of Frozone in the film *The Incredibles*.

2005: Appears in the *Guinness Book of World Records* as the top-grossing movie star at the box office.

2008: Appears in a special clip at the end of Iron Man as S.H.I.E.L.D. director Nick Fury; fan sites are soon abuzz at news he will play that role in a sequel.

Accomplishments/Awards
Selected Film Credits

Coming to America (1988)

Do the Right Thing (1989)

Mo' Better Blues (1990)

Jungle Fever (1991)

Patriot Games (1992)

Jurassic Park (1993)

Pulp Fiction (1994)

Die Hard with a Vengeance (1995)

Long Kiss Goodnight (1996)

Jackie Brown (1997)

Sphere (1998)

Star Wars: Episode One—The Phantom Menace (1999)

Shaft (2000)

Unbreakable (2000)

The 51st State (2001)

Star Wars: Episode Two—Attack of the Clones (2002)

S.W.A.T. (2003)

The Incredibles (2004)

Star Wars: Episode Three—Revenge of the Sith (2005)

Black Snake Moan (2006)

Snakes on a Plane (2006)

Cleaner (2007)

Awards

Cannes Film Festival, 1991

New York Film Critics Circle Awards, 1991

Kansas City Film Critics Circle Awards, 1992

BAFTA Awards, 1995

Independent Spirit Awards, 1995

Blockbuster Entertainment Awards, 1997

NAACP Image Awards, 1997

Acapulco Black Film Festival, 1998

Berlin International Film Festival, 1998

Independent Spirit Awards, 1998

Acapulco Black Film Festival, 1999

Hasty Pudding Theatricals, USA, 1999

Walk of Fame, 2000

BET Comedy Award, 2005

Bambi Award, 2006

NAACP Image Awards, 2006

Further Reading

Dils, Tracey E. *Samuel L. Jackson.* Minneapolis, Minn.: Sagebrush Educational Resources, 2000.

Hudson, Jeff. *Samuel L. Jackson: The King of Cool.* London: Virgin Books, 2004.

Internet Resources

http://samuelljackson.com/

Samuel L. Jackson's personal Web site.

http://www.imdb.com/name/nm0000168/

The Internet Movie Database contains biographical information about the actor, as well as lists of his movies and awards.

Glossary

addict—one who has an uncontrollable need for something, such as drugs.

audition—a tryout for a part in a movie or television or stage production; to try out for an acting role.

biopic—a movie depicting the real-life events of someone's life.

board of trustees—a group of people who guide and oversee an institution.

curriculum—a course of study for an academic degree; the combination of classes that one must take to understand a certain subject.

gross—the total amount of money taken in (before expenses are paid off).

maternal—on or from the mother's side of the family.

mentor—a person who helps and guides another person in his or her career.

prequel—a movie depicting events that take place before events depicted in a previously released film; the opposite of a sequel.

segregated—kept separated because of some characteristic, such as race (as in the southern United States before the civil rights movement).

Chapter Notes

p. 8: "The worst day I've ever . . ." Ian Watson, "Samuel L. Jackson," *Sunday Herald* (London), January 2003.

p. 9: "Don't recast me . . ." Margy Rochlin, "FILM; Tough Guy Finds His Warm and Fuzzy Side," *New York Times*, November 2, 1997.

p. 11: "Amazingly . . ." Dotson Rader, "He Found His Voice (Film Actor Samuel L. Jackson)," *Parade Magazine*, January 9, 2005. http://www.parade.com/articles/ editions/2005/edition_01-09-2005/featured_0

p. 13: "I had anger in me . . ." Ibid.

p. 15: "We were buying guns . . ." Ibid.

p. 19: "He was very . . ." Rochlin, "Tough Guy."

p. 19: "I decided that theater . . ." Rader, "He Found His Voice."

p. 22: "Actors act. I didn't . . ." Tavis Smiley interview with Samuel L. Jackson, *Tavis Smiley*, February 24, 2006.

p. 24: "He told me he was . . ." Rochlin, "Tough Guy."

p. 25: "My first big film . . ." Nasser Metcalfe, "Sept 99: Samuel L. Jackson's Actors Workshop," Blackfilm.com, September 1999. http://blackfilm.com/0109/features/workshop.shtml

p. 26: "I had never once . . ." Rader, "He Found His Voice."

p. 26: "There is no formula . . ." Oprah Winfrey, "King of Cool," *Oprah Winfrey Show*, January 16, 2006.

p. 28: "I have a very hard . . ." Lewis Beale, "Samuel L. Jackson

Went from Addict to Hollywood Star," *New York Daily News,* June 11, 2000. http://www.nydailynews.com/archives/entertainment/2000/06/11/2000-06-11_clean_break_with_the_past_sa.html

p. 30: "He has given me . . ." Ibid.

p. 31: "George Lucas told me . . ." "Samuel L. Jackson with 64 Movies to His Credit, Is Featured 'STAR WARS THE PHANTOM MENACE'," *Jet,* June 7, 1999. http://findarticles.com/p/articles/mi_m1355/is_1_96/ai_54968226

p. 33: "This has been the . . ." Rochlin, "Tough Guy."

p. 38: "All Sam does is . . ." Susan Wloszczyna, "Jackson the 'Snakes' Charmer," *USA Today,* August 16, 2006. http://www.usatoday.com/life/movies/news/2006-08-16-samuel-l-jackson_x.htm

p. 39: "I will pull . . ." Tavis Smiley interview with Samuel L. Jackson.

p. 40: "Golf is the one . . ." Beale, "Samuel L. Jackson."

p. 40: "My new drug . . ." Erich Leon Harris, "Lucky Star Samuel L. Jackson," *MovieMaker,* October 1, 1996. http://www.moviemaker.com/directing/article/lucky_star_samuel_l_jackson_3162/

p. 40: "It never occurs . . ." Oprah Winfrey interview with Samuel L. Jackson, *Oprah Winfrey Show,* January 16, 2006.

p. 40: "I don't consider myself . . ." Wloszczyna, " 'Snakes' Charmer."

p. 41: "I think I've made . . ." Rader, "He Found His Voice."

p. 43: "They're the same . . ." Eric Neel, "10 Burning Questions for . . . Samuel L. Jackson," *ESPN Page 2,* April 10, 2002. http://espn.go.com/page2/s/questions/samjackson.html

p. 43: "Some friends call . . ." Ibid.

p. 50: "And what was funny..." Charlie Rose, "Samuel L. Jackson," *The Charlie Rose Show,* October 22, 2002.

Index

Numbers in **bold italics** refer to captions.

Photo Credits

About the Authors

STACIA DEUTSCH AND RHODY COHON have written more than 21 books in the past four years. In addition to their award-winning creative chapter-book series, Blast to the Past, Stacia and Rhody also ghost write for a popular girl's mystery series, write nonfiction, and have a young adult romantic comedy novel called *In the Stars*. They have also written junior movie tie-in novels for summer blockbuster films, including *Batman, the Dark Knight*. Stacia lives in Irvine, California, with her three children. Rhody lives in Tucson, Arizona, with her three kids. Visit them at www.blasttothepastbooks.com.